The Litter Nutters

OTHER BOOKS BY BRIAN PATTEN

Brian Patten
The Utter Nutters

Illustrated by David Mostyn

PUFFIN BOOKS

PUFFIN BOOKS

Published by the Penguin Group
Penguin Books Ltd, 27 Wrights Lane, London W8 5TZ, England
Penguin Books USA Inc., 375 Hudson Street, New York, New York 10014, USA
Penguin Books Australia Ltd, Ringwood, Victoria, Australia
Penguin Books Canada Ltd, 10 Alcorn Avenue, Toronto, Ontario, Canada M4V 3B2
Penguin Books (NZ) Ltd, 182–190 Wairau Road, Auckland 10, New Zealand

Penguin Books Ltd, Registered Offices: Harmondsworth, Middlesex, England

First published by Viking 1994
Published in Puffin Books 1995
10 9 8 7 6 5 4 3 2

Made and printed in Great Britain by Clays Ltd, St Ives plc

THE UTTER NUTTERS' SONG

There's some utterly nutty nutters in our street,
They're the most utter nutty nutters that you'll meet.
　They're not just utter nutty,
　They're bonkers and quite batty,
They're the most utter nutty nutters that you'll meet.

Contents

Uncle Ben from Number One

Uncle Ben was not a hen
But when he laid an egg
He did it quite professionally
By lifting up a leg.

He studied it and prodded it
And said, 'I'm mystified.'
And then he took it to the kitchen
Where he had it, fried.

Mrs Cann from Number Two

THE PET HABIT FROM NUMBER FOUR

I'M FED UP PEOPLE TELLING ME
I'VE GOT A NASTY HABIT.
BUT I HAVE. IT'S TRUE. I DO.

GULP!

I KEEP IT IN A BOX FULL OF DIRTY STRAW.
I FEED IT NOSE-PICKINGS AND BELCHES,
BITS OF SPIT AND BUM-SCRATCHES.
IT'S A NASTY LITTLE HABIT.
WHEN PEOPLE ASK, 'WHAT'S IN THAT BOX?'
I SAY, 'IT'S MY PET HABIT.'
'DON'T YOU MEAN PET RABBIT?' THEY ASK.
'NO,' I SAY, AND SHOW THEM.
'THAT'S A NASTY LITTLE HABIT,' THEY SAY.

Why Victor's Mum Vanished from Number Five

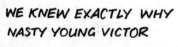

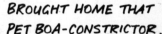

Alice Frip from Number Six

Peering down the sewer
Gave Alice Frip a fright—
There was something slimy
Down there out of sight.

Nameless things floated by,

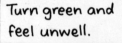
I'M A MOUSE WITH NO NAME.

And of course the smell
Made her next-door neighbours

Turn green and feel unwell.

They had all decided
Poor Alice Frip was mad,
And her unhealthy fascination
Pathetic and quite sad.

And agreed this was not so,
For something nasty grabbed her,
And dragged her down below.

Grandad from Number Seven

Once Grandad was my age
(Or so he's often said).
I wonder, when he was eight
Did he smoke a pipe in bed?
On his way to junior school
Did he forget his teeth?
And did he use a zimmer-frame
To jog around the heath?
Was he ever really young?
If so, did he used to pop
Out the classroom every day
To the pub and betting-shop?
Did he chew gum with his gums?
Did he scare the school bully
Simply by standing round
Looking old and smelly?

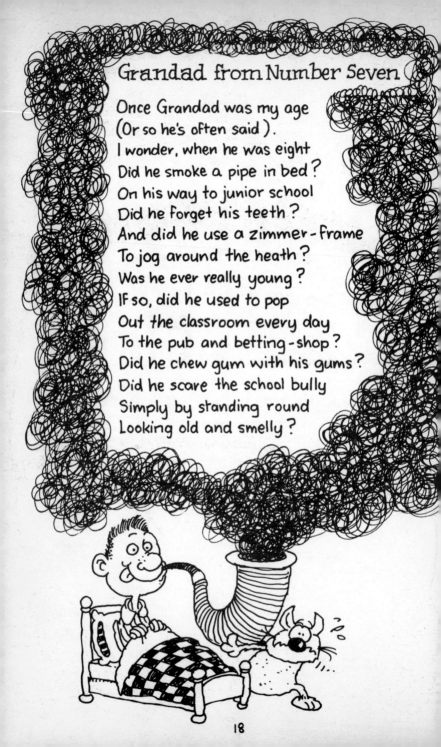

GREEDYGUTS

FROM NUMBER EIGHT

A giraffe's a giraffe,
An ape is an ape,
But Henry is a pig
In a different shape.

19

The Lone Wolf from Number Nine

The man from number nine
Never spoke,
Was known as
'The quiet bloke'.
He'd smile or nod,
No more than that.
Silent as snow
He'd come and go,
Dip in and out
The street's life.
'A lone wolf,' Gran said.
At night I imagined him
Howling at the moon
Or pacing beneath stars.
A lone wolf behind
The street's rough bars.

THE PIRATE'S ARMPIT

The official Official
Who comes to our street
Is sleek and neat.
Dad says
He's a twit.
Dad says

With him around
You'd need a permit
To smell
A pirate's armpit.

Some of Old Mother Wise's Sayings (from Number Ten)

Like bees to honey
kids to pocket-money

HONEY | POCKET MONEY

Nothing's cleaner
Than a ballerina

A stolen rose smells of fish

BEDTIME WAS
INVENTED BY ADULTS
THE MOMENT THEY
FORGOT THEY WERE
EVER CHILDREN

From the mouths of the venomous
All fibs are poisonous

The truth fluctuates
according to the damage
done

I DON'T SPEAK WITH A FORKED TONGUE, HONEST

EH? ....

PHILIP O'FROWT FROM NUMBER 11

Young Philip O'Frowt
Was a terrible lout,
At night he would creep
Up into his sister's bedroom
When she was fast asleep.

He had some spiders
And he had some frogs
(He really wasn't nice),
He had lots of toads
And a bag of worms,
And he had some wriggly mice.

23

THE BOGEYMAN AT NUMBER TWELVE

The man in the darkness on the top stair
Is always pretending not to be there

Deep in the dark on the very top stair.

The man in the darkness on the top stair
Whispers so quietly only I hear

His voice in the darkness on the top stair.

And I'm never certain that it's him there,
For the man in the dark on the top stair

Is shadowy faint and thin as the air.

And when the dawn creeps up to the top stair,
I can never work out exactly where

He stood in the darkness on the top stair.

He can vanish like stars, like mist into air,
And leave only a black cat licking its fur,

Curled up in the sunlight on the top stair.

MY SISTER'S BLISTER (AT NUMBER THIRTEEN)

MY SISTER HAS A BLISTER
ON A SPOT THAT A SISTER
WOULDN'T SAY SHE HAD A BLISTER,
AND SO MY SISTER'S BLISTER
IS A SECRET KIND OF BLISTER,
AND AT DINNER-TIME MY SISTER
SAYS NOTHING OF HER BLISTER
BUT SUPS HER SOUP WHILE STANDING
AND SAYS IT'S LESS DEMANDING.
SHE'S A SILLY KIND OF SISTER
AND IT'S HARD TO RESIST A
LITTLE POKE AT THAT BLISTER
ON THE BOTTOM OF MY SISTER.

GROGGY MOGGY
JEKYLL HYDE

Leon Peabody
from Number Fourteen

A puppy belonging to Leon
Spent all day attempting to pee on
Mrs Fry who would cry,
'I must ask Leon why
I'm the only one his puppy'll pee on!'

Dusty Madge from Number Fifteen

Madge would polish things for hour upon hour.
'You need sun-glasses in her house,'
Mum always said.

The smell of polish
Wafted from her window
Like scent from a wooden flower.

Madge, widowed and alone,
Polished her fingers
To the bone.

But no matter how much Madge cleaned
The dust rose from the dead,
Returned as if it belonged.

She'd sweep the pavement,
Scrub the window-sill and shout
If you stepped on her doorstep.

'But everything's clean,' I'd whisper.
'Hush,' Mum would reply. 'Be kind.
The dust is in her mind.'

NO.
15

LAZY LARRY FROM
NUMBER SIXTEEN

TURNER TEVEY

TURNER TEVEY'S DROWNED?
WHAT'S THAT, MUM? I CAN'T HEAR YOU!
I DON'T KNOW ANY TURNER TEVEY.
WHERE DID SHE DROWN, MUM?
WHAT'S THAT, MUM? I CAN'T HEAR YOU.
IN ASAID TERNIROV?
WHERE'S ASAID TERNIROV?

I DON'T KNOW ANY RUSSIAN PLACES.
ANYWAY, WHAT WAS TURNER TEVEY DOING IN
        ASAID TERNIROV?
WHAT'S THAT, MUM? IN DOOSYETOLED?
I THOUGHT YOU SAID TURNER TEVEY
DROWNED IN ASAID TERNIROV, NOT DOOSYETOLE
WHAT'S THAT, MUM? AH, I SEE,

OK,
I'LL TURN THE TV DOWN, AND
DO AS I'M TOLD.

MR PIKE

FROM NUMBER SEVENTEEN

MR PIKE WAS NOT A FISH,

HE COULDN'T EVEN SWIM.

HELP!

WE KNEW THAT STAYING UNDER WATER WOULD BE THE DEATH OF HIM.

WEEP

SOB!

DEEP GRIEF

HE WAS NOT A ROACH,

HE WAS NOT A COD,

NOPE!

A SALMON

OR A TROUT,

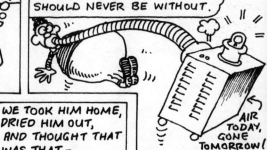
AIR WAS SOMETHING MR PIKE SHOULD NEVER BE WITHOUT.

AIR TODAY, GONE TOMORROW!

ONE DAY HE TOOK A DEEP BREATH AND BEING QUITE A FOOL DIVED NEATLY FROM A GREAT HEIGHT INTO A SHALLOW POOL.

BOING!

WE TOOK HIM HOME, DRIED HIM OUT, AND THOUGHT THAT WAS THAT - BUT LATE AT NIGHT POOR MR PIKE WAS STOLEN BY THE CAT!

HELP

17

TOOTHSOME TITTER!

Lazy Lizzy's Baby

from number eighteen

Lazy Lizzy's baby cried
And then began to sigh,
For into its tiny mouth
Had flown a juicy fly.
Slowly it digested it,
And that's the reason why...

The baby staggered to its feet.
It began to crawl.

AUNTIE?

It climbed right up the skirting board
Outside in the hall.
It climbed across a painting.

It climbed up the wall.
It clung on to the ceiling.
We thought it must fall.

We bribed it with sugar cubes.

We spoke darkly of glue

GLUE

We threatened it with spiders —

We discussed what to do.

IT'S ONE OF US!!

Then while we all stood gaping
It sprouted tiny wings.
Rough hairs grew on its back legs.
They were disgusting things.

We tried to use a
fly-swat.

We tried to use
a spray.

We tried to
get it back
down
Before it
flew away.

Then suddenly we noticed
The windows open wide.

'Shut them, quickly!' Lizzie
said,
'Or it'll get outside.'

But the baby sensed its freedom,
And as if on cue
It flicked its wings and buzzed about,
And then off it flew.

MRS RABARUA FROM NUMBER NINETEEN

Ever optimistic
Mrs Rabarua
Fished down the sewer.
She'd take off the manhole cover,
Drop her bait, and wait.

And wait.

And wait.

And wait.

'These days
There are fewer
Down the sewer,'
Sighed Mrs Rabarua.

Toffee-nosed Paula from 20

Spotless, unblemished, poised and correct,
Toffee-nosed Paula would often get vexed.

She'd slip in a place you'd never expect
Aunt Mary's dog to stop and reflect.

Toffee-nosed Paula, unblemished, correct,
Thought Aunt Mary's dog had a major defect.

The Pussy-owl at Number 21

What's that? A cat?
What? That? A cat?!
Not that!
A fowl or owl but
It's no cat - not that!

Oh, I see.
Max came for tea.
He brought a tube of glue.
Did he bring those feathers too?
No? Then who?

The cat's to blame?
It ripped a pillow with its claws?
It rolled in the glue?
Then it rolled
In the feathers too?

What? You don't think
It should be called a cat?
I agree with that. What's tha
It goes, 'Mew-wooo, mew-wooo
So it's become an owl-cat now?

If it's so rare why look so glum
Oh, I see.
Here comes your mum...

38

Misery Miser from Number Twenty-Two

Dried-up pens and empty cans,
Papers from the distant past,
I keep them in a corner
Where they last, and last, and last.

My tatty vest is threadbare,
All my underwear is damp.
Because I wash it in the soup
I often get the cramp.

Just in case a hungry guest
Demands some food to chew on
I've put aside ancient pies
And something green with fluff on.

SELL
BY
30/4/87

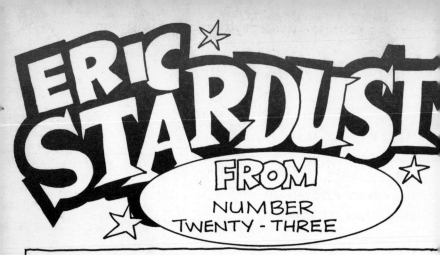

ERIC STARDUST

FROM
NUMBER TWENTY - THREE

It depressed Eric Stardust's poor mum

When her son went and borrowed a drum

He bashed it and crashed it

And so his dad smashed it.

Now it's Eric who's glum not his mum.

 Rumours

SUNG BY THE HIPPY FROM NUMBER TWENTY-FOUR

There's a rumour the stars have just frozen
(God left His fridge open again).
Robots and mice like them like ice,
Then they melt, and turn into rain.

There's a rumour the leaves have a language
That they learn when merely a bud.
I overheard that it's taught by a bird
With a beak the colour of blood.

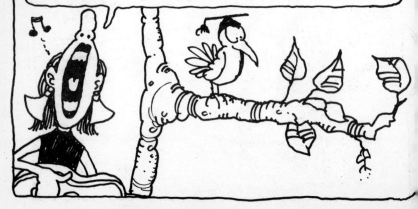

I've been told there's a crack that the daylight
Leaks through at the end of each day.
Nobody knows quite where it goes,
And can't stop it draining away.

There's a rumour the ocean's been taken
And hung up on a line to dry.
In the heights of the Atlantic Ocean
Satellites and angels drift by.

Every day I hear dozens of rumours -
They buzz and they bumble about.
Ninety-nine per cent are absurd,
And about the rest there's a doubt.

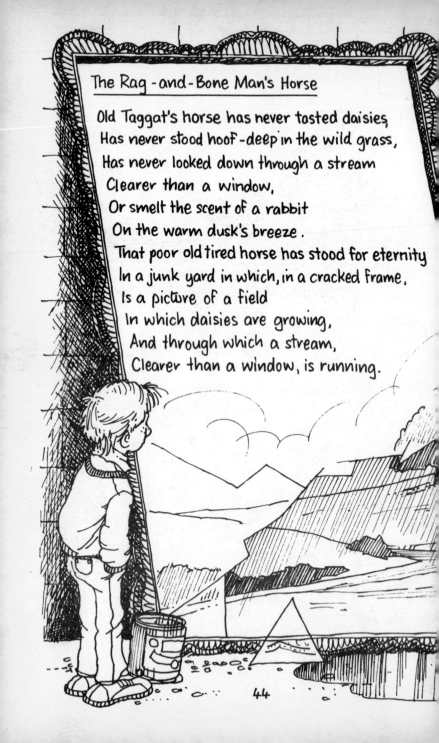

The Rag-and-Bone Man's Horse

Old Taggat's horse has never tasted daisies,
Has never stood hoof-deep in the wild grass,
Has never looked down through a stream
Clearer than a window,
Or smelt the scent of a rabbit
On the warm dusk's breeze.
That poor old tired horse has stood for eternity
In a junk yard in which, in a cracked frame,
Is a picture of a field
In which daisies are growing,
And through which a stream,
Clearer than a window, is running.

45.

PLAYING THE BABY

AT NUMBER TWENTY-FIVE

WHEN I WANT TO PLAY MUSIC LOUD
PEOPLE COMPLAIN:

'TURN THAT !@>#*! MUSIC DOWN

IT'S A PAIN.
IT GETS ME DOWN BECAUSE

WHEN THE WOMAN NEXT DOOR
WANTS TO PLAY HER BABY LOUD,
IF I SHOUT, **'TURN THAT BABY DOWN!'**

GUESS WHAT?

NOTHING HAPPENS.

How Not to Have to Mend Your Bike at Number Twenty-Six

'Use your loaf!' my father said-
'Is there nothing in your head?

Use your brains - is that grey matter
Just so much cooking batter.

Use your noodle,
your common sense-
Are you really quite
so dense?

Where's the manual?
Can't you read!
That spanner's not
what you need.

OK, OK, just this once
I'll fix your bike -
you're such a dunce!'

ALL THIS PROVES I'M FAR TOO BRAINY TO MEND MY BIKE WHEN IT'S RAINY.

A BIRD, DROPPING

There's no stopping
A bird dropping.

The Murder at No. 27

Mr Jones made me shudder.
He made his wife
Quiver with terror.

Just looking at him
Made your flesh creep
Off into a corner.

He was a rat.
One night Mrs Jones
Put down the bait.

Rat bait. Which he ate.

MUM SAYS,
IF YOU PLEASE!
THOSE FLEAS
AREN'T OURS.

DAD SAYS,
WHERE'D THEY COME FROM –
MARS?

YEP!

MUM SAYS,
AND THAT MOUSE
ISN'T FROM OUR HOUSE!

DAD SAYS,
ARE THE MICE AND FLEAS
TAKING HOLIDAYS?

MUM SAYS,
AND THAT STINK!
IT'S NOT FROM OUR SINK.

I SAY NOTHING.
I'VE HEARD IT ALL BEFORE –
BLAMING THEM NEXT DOOR.

ADVANTAGEOUS CONTAGIOUS AT No.29

I hate lying in bed with measles
Even more than they hate lying in bed with me.

I'm fed up with books and comics,
There's only romantic yuk on TV.
Every five minutes the clock stops for a rest

BUT...

Because it's exam time
And a bully from another school is looking for me
And because I owe everyone money
And because the last gigantic lie I told
Has just been discovered,
I'm lying low.

Sometimes
It's advantageous
TO BE
CONTAGIOUS

BULLY BABY

FROM NUMBER THIRTY

DON'T YOU COME NEAR ME,

I'M SCARY, I'M HAIRY,

I'M A BULLY, A BIFFER, I'M FOUL.

AND WHATEVER YOU DO

DON'T YELL OR SHOUT BOO

OR I'LL RUN TO MY (MUMMY) AND HOWL.

Ma-Ma!
Ma-Ma!
Ma-Ma!

THERE'S MORE BABIES AT NUMBER 31

Babies, God bless them, are bags full of noises
Around which clever people have sewn
A lot of pink skin, a bib and a bonnet
To which they have added a large megaphone.

Babies, please bless them, are bags full of noises,
Useful as foghorns and sirens and such.
They are best put out at night in the garden,
And that's why I'm making a new rabbit hutch.

Babies, I tell you, are bags full of noises,
They burp, they gurgle, they cry and they belch,
And if you put them down on a hard surface
Their nappies can make a horrible squelch.

RIDDLE

'Your father was my father's son;
Though sons and brothers have I none.
Tell me, please, and please tell me true.
What's my relationship to you?'

56

The Cosmic Disaster from Number 33

The girl down the road's a moan,
A misery, a mess –
She always seems to be
In terrible distress.

A cut is never just a cut,
It's a cosmic disaster.
We don't know what she looks like –
She's always wrapped in plaster.

WHAT A BORING BROTHER THAT BORING BROTHER IS (AT NUMBER THIRTY-FOUR)

He's peevish,

impatient,

grumpy and gruff

And sometimes I think, Enough is enough!

I'll pack him in ice,

preserve him in brine,

I'll magic away that brother of mine.

KAZOOM!!

Down the drain with his fingers!

In the bin with his toes!

On to a tip with his fat little nose!

His body is chewy, a treat for a bear!

Toss the rest of him wherever you care -
Just keep him away!
Enough is enough!
(If I see him again I'm going to get tough.)

Some more of Old Mother Wise's Sayings

ADULTS ARE CHILDREN WHO HAVE CALMED DOWN

POCKET-MONEY IS LIKE REAL MONEY ONLY NOT AS MUCH

ADULTS NEED MORE SLEEP THAN CHILDREN BECAUSE THEY ARE NEVER QUITE AS AWAKE

THE DIFFERENCE BETWEEN A FIB AND A LIE IS THAT A FIB MIGHT GET YOU OUT OF TROUBLE, BUT A LIE WILL ALWAYS GET SOMEONE ELSE INTO TROUBLE.

TOYS ARE MADE BY ADULTS AND SOLD IN SHOPS OWNED BY ADULTS, BUT CHILDREN STILL GET THE BLAME WHEN THEY ARE EXPENSIVE

ONLY CHILDREN KNOW THE NUTRITIONAL VALUE OF SWEETS

MR MCGUIRE FROM NUMBER 35

OLD MR MCGUIRE, BLIND AS A BAT,

HAD A RABBIT, A WEASEL, A DOG AND A CAT.

HE STROKED THEM ALL AS HE SAT BY THE FIRE,

SOME DAYS THEY FELT SMOOTH,

AND SOME DAYS LIKE WIRE.

WITH A BARK, A HISS, A SQUEAK AND MIAOW

THEY DEMANDED ATTENTION

AND ALL GOT IT SOMEHOW.

OLD MR MCGUIRE, HE LOVED THEM ALL –

'TO ME YOU'RE ONE CREATURE

YOU'RE ALL FROM THE SAME SACK.

GOD BROUGHT YOU HERE

AND HE'LL TAKE YOU BACK.

YOU MAY THINK YOU'RE ALL DIFFERENT

BUT, HEAVENS ABOVE –

YOU ARE ALL OF YOU LOVED

WITH ONE SINGLE LOVE.'

Windy Granny from Number 36

What is that unearthly sound I hear—
Those peculiar whistles?
Could it be the north wind
Blowing through Granny's bristles?

SCREEEE

HUUMMMMMMM

WWOOOOOOO

weeeeeeeee

THRUUMMMM M M

Gran's Old Fox Fur Coat

Manky, rank, damp and tainted.
When Granny put it on I almost fainted.
It's made of hair from a gorilla's nostril
And is older than the oldest pterodactyl.

63

Leon Peabody Told Me a Secret

How secret's a secret? I want to know.
The one I've been keeping I have to let go.
It's making me burst, it's such a strain
Having a big secret locked up in my brain.
How secret's a secret? How long must it stay
Hidden inside me, bubbling away?

My tongue's in a knot, my jaws really ache,
It's late in the night but I'm wide awake.
Is there a limit on how long they last?
If so let me know when the limit has passed!
Secrets are time bombs, they can't help but blow.
If you have one keep silent - I don't want to know!

SUE FURST

from the cafe on the corner

This is a picture of Sue Furst
A few moments after she burst.
It was the final crumb
On its way through her tum
That's the one she has always cursed.

Mr Bone
from
Number
Thirty - Seven

Mr Bone,
Old as a dinosaur,
Was a bit of a bore.

If you weren't fleet
He'd catch you in the street

And go on and
Zzzzzzzzz on.
Mr Bone,
Prone to drone.

Lived alone.

Belinda

from Number Thirty-Eight

'The oven's haunted!'
Moaned Belinda,
Burning dinner
To a cinder.
Only Belinda
Could roast
A ghost,
Cook
A spook.

Nice and Nasty from Number Thirty-nine

A pair of twins live down the road,
But I never know which is which -
I'm often nice to the nasty one
And push the nice one in a ditch.
Then the nice one says I'm nasty
And the nasty one says I'm nice -
But I was only nasty to the nice one
Because I thought the nasty one was nice.

THE STUFFED Pixie

AT NO.40

The world's last pixie sat in the street
Playing with a golden ball,

A ten-ton lorry crushed it
But it felt no pain at all.*

*The lorry that is, not the poor pixie

I took it home, had it stuffed,

And put it in the corner,

And to make it feel at home

I surrounded it with fauna.*

* That's fauna's flora!

AMBROSE

FROM NUMBER FORTY-ONE

NOTHING COULD EVER ENCLOSE

AMBROSE,

OR TRANQUILLIZE OR HYPNOTIZE

AMBROSE.

AMBROSE, ON HIS OWN,

A ONE-MAN WAR-ZONE.

WHEREVER HE GOES
CUPS AND PLATES FALL

LIKE ROWS
OF DOMINOES

AMBROSE,
A TANK ON TOES.

HYPERACTIVE, I SUPPOSE,
IS AMBROSE.

First Snow in the Street

I did not sleep last night.
The falling snow was beautiful and white.
I dressed, sneaked down the stairs
And opened wide the door.
I had not seen such snow before.

Our grubby little street had gone;
The world was brand-new and everywhere
There was a pureness in the air.
I felt such peace. Watching every flake
I felt more and more awake.

I thought I'd learned all there was to know
About the trillion million different kinds
Of swirling frosty falling flakes of snow.
But that was not so.
I did not know how vividly it lit
The world with such a peaceful glow.

Upstairs my parents slept.
I could not drag myself away from that sight
To call them down and have them share
The mute miracle of the snow.
It seemed to fall for me alone.
How beautiful the grubby little street had grown!

Gentrification

Posh wardrobe

OLD BOY
NETWORK
REMOVALS

BY APPOINTMENT
TO EVERYONE

Posh salu...

Posh red carpet

Another posh couple,
with airs and graces,
stuck-up noses
and snooty faces,
have just moved in.

The shop on the corner,
with its bits and pieces,
its dusty boxes
and choc-ices,
has closed.

Neighbours we used to think
were daft or a bore
have become our friends now -
even the nuts next door.